Sweet Crochet

By Sandrine Deveze
Photos by Cinqmai

PETER PAUPER PRESS, INC.
White Plains, New York

Contents

Introduction

I discovered the wonderful world of crochet quite recently, falling under the spell of the numerous stunning, brightly-colored crocheted blankets that were all over the pages of interior decorating magazines and blogs. I tried my hardest to make them myself—but as a hopelessly impatient person, I never managed to finish any of my projects. The ambitious blanket projects quickly became simple pillows. Soon, however, I discovered that crochet was not limited to clothing and accessories. I fell in love with designer Anne-Claire Petit's creative universe filled with unique hand-crocheted toys, and then with *amigurumi:* tiny crocheted (or knitted) animals filled with wool or commercial stuffing, which became the hallmarks of Japanese crochet art. These projects could be completed much more quickly, and were much more accessible, than any crochet project I had previously attempted.

I'm self-taught at crochet. I have no memory of watching my grandmothers or my mother crochet. However, I clearly remember many long, happy evenings spent with my crochet hook and a ball of cotton thread. My notebooks overflowed with notes and tips garnered here and there. I also spent many hours reading blogs and watching videos, under the baffled eye of my partner, as I strove to understand the subtleties of single, double, and double-treble stitches. At first I thought I would never get the hang of it, and spent countless hours undoing and redoing my work, but I persevered. I still remember my very first completed crochet project: a red apple. After that there was no stopping me! It became an absolute passion and a fantastic way to relax after a tough day at work. Now I look for any excuse to crochet: a baby shower gift, a birthday present... and of course, my three children's beds are covered with *amigurumi!*

Through this book I hope to share my passion for crochet. The best advice I can give you is just to try it out. Take a quiet moment, sit in your favorite chair with a fresh cup of tea at your side, grab your crochet hook and a ball of cotton yarn, and begin! Don't be afraid to make mistakes. Crochet is best learned by practice. Errors are useful, and will speed your learning. You don't need to strive for perfection; dropping a stitch here or there is no big deal. Besides, it's often these small mistakes that imbue handcrafted projects with their trademark charm.

Sandrine Deveze

MATERIALS
and
TECHNIQUES

MATERIALS

In general, you'll need only a crochet hook and yarn or thread to complete most of your work. This means you can crochet virtually anywhere, anytime! You can also add a few accessories to these two basics.

★ Yarns

The thickness and texture of the yarn/ thread you use will determine your character's final dimensions. The thicker the yarn, the bigger the *amigurumi*, and vice-versa.

I often advise beginners to start with #3 (4-ply, 3/2, or fingering weight) or #4 cotton yarns. Your stitches will be more visible and easier to count. 100% cotton yarns are easy to work and perfect for *amigurumi* crochet projects, as cotton fibers don't stretch much and will not warp when stuffed. Moreover, this yarn is ideal for creating children's toys, as it is low-maintenance, wear-and-tear-resistant, and machine-washable.

I have chosen to work with Natura Just Cotton crochet thread by DMC (1). I also use DMC's Lumina line of metallic threads for some projects, as well as pearl cotton floss from this same manufacturer.

Once you are comfortable with crochet techniques, you can try using different types of yarns and threads to change the look of your toys.

Try mohair for a fluffier look or wool for a softer texture. For a mottled, heathery look, work up your projects with two strands of yarn or thread at a time (doubled) using one strand of white pearl cotton floss (as seen in patterns like **Sushi Platter!** on page 24 and **Wolfgang** on page 51, for example). If your thread is very fine, continue working with a size 3 crochet hook; otherwise, you can move to a size 4.

TIP: *If you choose to work with crochet thread other than those in the Natura Just Cotton product line, make sure their technical specifications are similar to the following: 100% cotton, 50 grams (1.75 oz), +/- 155 m (170 yards), requires a 2.5 mm or 3.0 mm crochet hook. Depending on where you buy your cotton thread, #3 cotton may be referred to as 3/2. To obtain a 10 x 10 cm (4" x 4") square, the stitch gauge should be approximately 27 stitches x 34 rows or rounds.*

★ Crochet Hooks

Crochet hooks are available in a variety of sizes and materials (metal, bamboo, plastic, etc.). To make these little characters, I frequently use a 3.0 mm metal crochet hook (2), and very occasionally a 1.5 mm or 6.0 mm hook (3) to make small accessories or when using a doubled thread. Clover brand hooks are extremely ergonomic and have an excellent hand feel. They are easy to find. User preferences vary, however, so it's best to try several types and choose the brand and model that feels right to you.

When creating *amigurumi*, stitches should be as tight as possible. If you tend to crochet loosely, it would be best to use a smaller (by 0.5 mm to 1 mm) crochet hook, rather than follow the guidelines listed on the skein. This way you can obtain tighter stitches and also prevent the stuffing from being visible between the stitches, which will affect the toy's overall look.

Safety Eyes

Until recently it was difficult to find plastic safety eye clips (4) in some areas. However, they are beginning to appear on the shelves in select craft stores or online shops (see page 64) in a wide assortment of colors (red, blue, green, orange, etc.) and sizes. There are even accessories (noses, snouts, etc.).

NOTE: *Safety eyes are not suitable for children under age 3. When making an amigurumi for a baby, it's best to create the eyes with black embroidery thread.*

★ Basic Kit

Here is a handy checklist of frequently-needed items when making *amigurumi*:

- A tapestry or wool needle (5) to assemble the various individually-crocheted parts. These needles have round tips and very large eyes to facilitate the insertion of the different threads used to create the pieces;
- A classic sewing needle (6) may also be used with sewing thread to join smaller pieces or to embroider facial features;
- A doll needle (7). This is a very long, fine 12.5 cm (5") needle with a large eye, especially suited for cotton thread;
- A pair of scissors (8);
- A tape measure (9);
- A stitch marker or paper clip (10) to identify the first stitch in each row;
- A red drawing pencil (11) and a fabric scrap (12) to color in your characters' cheeks;
- Kapok or synthetic, anti–dust mite stuffing (13). Natural carded wool can also be used if you want your *amigurumi* to be made with 100% natural fibers.

BASIC STITCHES TO USE

CHAIN STITCH(ES): CH(S)

1. Make a slip knot by wrapping the yarn around the hook, then slipping it back through the loop. Leave a long tail to weave in when your project is done.

2. Yarn over and then pull it back through the loop. To make a chain—the starting point of any crochet project—use this method to cast on the required number of chain stitches. Note, however, that the loop on the hook should not be counted as a stitch.

SLIP STITCH(ES): SL ST(S)

1. Insert the hook into the 2nd stitch on the chain.

2. Yarn over and then pull it through both loops. In most patterns, this stitch will be used mainly to finish the work.

SINGLE CROCHET: SC

1. Push the hook through the 2nd stitch on the chain.

2. Yarn over and then pull it through one loop.

3. Yarn over again and then pull it through both loops.

Yarn over: *"Yarn over" (abbreviated as "yo") is the act of looping the yarn around the hook, either before or after inserting the hook into a stitch.*

DOUBLE CROCHET(S): DC

1. Yarn over and push the hook through the 4th stitch in the chain.

2. Yarn over again and then pull it through one loop.

3. Yarn over again and then pull it through two loops.

4. Yarn over for the last time and then pull it through both remaining loops.

DOUBLE TREBLE: DTR

1. Yarn over twice, and push the hook through the 5th stitch in the chain.

2. Yarn over again and then pull the hook through one loop.

3. Yarn over again and then pull the hook through two loops.

4. Yarn over again and then pull the hook through two loops.

5. Yarn over for the final time and then pull the hook through both remaining loops.

INCREASE: INC

Make two single crochet stitches in the same stitch.

DECREASE: DEC

1. Join two single crochet stitches into one. To do so, push the hook through the first stitch, yarn over, and pull the yarn through the stitch. You will now have 2 loops on the hook.

2. Insert the hook into the next stitch, yarn over, and pull the yarn through the stitch. You will now have 3 loops on the hook.

3. Yarn over and pull the yarn through all 3 loops

ABBREVIATIONS CHECKLIST

Chain stitch	ch	**Double treble**	dtr
Single crochet	sc	**Stitch**	st
Slip stitch	sl st	**Increase**	inc
Double crochet	dc	**Decrease**	dec

BASIC TECHNIQUES

★ Starting a project

Amigurumi are generally worked in the round using single crochet (sc) stitches. Your stitching should be very tight, to ensure the stuffing remains invisible. You should therefore master the single crochet and the chain stitch (ch).

The first three rounds are the most delicate. Once these steps have been mastered, the rest will be easy. Make sure to carefully read through the entire pattern before beginning your project.

There are many techniques for starting a project. Some prefer the magic ring technique, while others begin with a slip knot. I always make two chain stitches and use the first to work around.

Amigurumi are created from several crocheted pieces, which are then stuffed and assembled. Each piece begins with a central loop (or magic ring), around which single crochet stitches are added counter-clockwise. Next, a series of increases and decreases will give the piece its final shape. Instructions for each piece are listed in rounds. First, you will find the round number, then the instructions and the number of stitches you should have at the end of each round (which will allow you to easily check for errors or forgotten stitches).

When an instruction must be repeated several times within a given round, it is noted between two asterisks. This notation helps keep the instructions clear and simple. Perform the required actions once, then repeat them the number of times indicated.

Example: Round 3: *sc 1 in the next st, inc 1 in the next st*, repeat 5 more times from * to * (= 18 sc).

However, some elements must be crocheted "back and forth." In that case I will refer to "rows". Beginning with a basic chain, create horizontal lines of single crochet stitches by working forward and then back. Finish each row with a chain stitch, and turn your work over.

★ Placing a marker

Amigurumi are always crocheted in the round or in a spiral. Therefore, the end of the round should not be closed off with a slip stitch. Marking the start of each round is essential; otherwise, it will be nearly impossible to find your place, and you will find yourself constantly counting stitches. To place a marker, insert a piece of thread, in a contrasting color and about ten centimeters (4 inches) long, at the start of the round, and move this thread as you work through the pattern. You can also use a paper clip, a safety pin, or a ring marker.

Sample instructions for the first six rounds of a pattern:

1. Make a 2 ch chain. First, start by looping the yarn around the hook.

2. Yarn over and pull the yarn through the loop. You have just created your first chain stitch (ch).

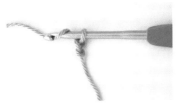

3. Repeat this step once more to make a 2nd ch.

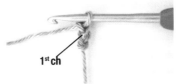

1st ch

4. Loosen the 1st ch.

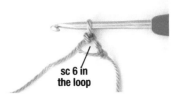

sc 6 in the loop

Round 1: sc 6 in this 1st ch

5. Tighten the loop.

Round 2: Insert the hook into the 1st sc of previous round.

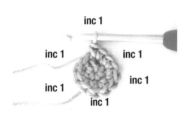

6. inc 1 in each sc of previous round (= 12 sc).

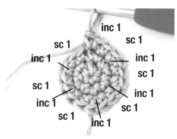

Round 3: *sc 1 in the next stitch, then inc 1 in the next stitch*, repeat 5 more times from * to * (= 18 sc).

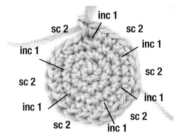

Round 4: *sc 2, inc 1*, repeat 5 more times from * to * (=24 sc).

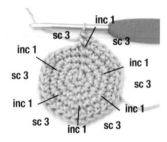

Round 5: *sc 3, inc 1*, repeat 5 more times from * to * (= 30 sc).

Round 6: sc 1 in each sc of previous round (= 30 sc).

7. As soon as you stop increasing, you will notice the edges beginning to curve up.

8. Next, begin to decrease when noted in the instructions. The principle is the same as for increases: alternate single crochet stitches and decreases. At the end of the last round, use a slip stitch to bind off the work and make a knot. Cut the thread, leaving a tail approximately 20 cm (8") long for assembly or weaving in.

Tip: *Try stuffing your amigurumi as you go.*

you to weave the ends of the embroidery thread inside the head. You should always embroider facial features with the face fully stuffed.

Your *amigurumi's* face will be even cuter if you lightly color the cheeks. To do so, take a small piece of fabric and a red pencil. Press the pencil forcefully onto the fabric to color it, then gently rub the fabric around your character's cheeks. As a precaution, you can test out the process on a small crocheted square in the same color before applying it to your work.

★ Assembly

To assemble the so-called "open" pieces like the head and torso, thread the tapestry needle with the tail of the yarn used for the head. Make sure the head is positioned correctly atop the body. Insert the needle into one of the last body stitches, pull slightly, then reinsert in one of the last head stitches. Repeat this process as many times as necessary. When you have gone around the head, make a knot. Go through the body with the needle, pull slightly, and then cut the yarn short. When the tension is released, the yarn will disappear into the body.

To sew the so-called "closed" pieces like the arms, legs, and ears, pin the edges side by side, with stitches facing each other. Thread the yarn through the tapestry needle. Insert the needle slightly in front of the first stitch, and then slightly in front of the facing stitch. Repeat this process for the entire round. Next, sew the closed piece onto your character. You can also close the piece with a round of single crochet stitches by inserting the hook into both facing stitches at the same time.

★ Weaving in ends

When your piece is finished, make a slip stitch to close off the work. Cut the yarn, leaving a tail roughly 20 cm (8") long. Thread the yarn into the tapestry needle and make a small hidden stitch. Go through the body with the needle, pull slightly, and then cut the yarn short. When the tension is released, the yarn will disappear into the body.

★ Changing yarns

You will often need to change yarns, either because the instructions require that you switch colors or because you run out of yarn. In all cases, change yarns at the end of a round. Start your final stitch as you usually would, then make your final yarn over (yo) with the new yarn. Continue working normally. After four stitches with the new yarn, knot the two tails together. You can later hide the knot inside your work.

★ Creating the face

While this is one of the most important and painstaking steps in your project, it can also be the most satisfying. It is at this point that your character's full personality will emerge.

Always begin with the eyes. Before attaching them to the face, firmly stuff the head so you have a clear idea of its final dimensions. Follow the instructions regarding placement of the eyes, nose, and/or mouth in each chapter. Position each element and mark its exact location with a paper clip or a faint pencil mark. Remove one third of the stuffing.

Plastic safety eyes, visible in the **Materials** photo on page 5, are made up of two parts. The first is visible (the black post) and the other is hidden within the character (the metal or plastic disc). First, insert the black post in the appropriate spot. Turn your work over and push the plastic/metal disc onto the base of the black post. The discs are usually difficult to place properly, so feel free to force it on. You can also use a pair of pliers if necessary.

Once these have been placed, firmly stuff the head once again. Before joining it to the torso, embroider the mouth and/or nose. This will allow

• LITTLE OWLS •

With their big round eyes and their prettily-decorated tummies, these little owls will surely get lots of attention! They suit equally well as decorative features, hung onto tree branches, or tied to a mobile, swinging gently above Baby's crib. This pattern is specially tailored for beginners.

DIFFICULTY LEVEL: ★ — DIMENSIONS OF AN OWL: 9 X 5.5 CM (3.5" X 2.25")

★ Materials

For one owl:
1 ball size 3 grey cotton crochet thread
1 ball size 3 white cotton crochet thread
Red and white sewing thread
1 crochet hook – 3.0 mm
2 plastic safety eyes, black, 6 mm
Basic kit (see page 5)

★ Stitches

Chain stitch (ch)
Single crochet stitch (sc)
Slip stitch (sl st)

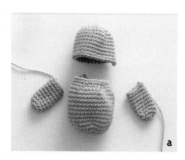

a

Instructions

1. Use the grey colorway for the head.

Round 1: ch 2, then add 6 sc in the 1st ch.

Round 2: inc 1 in each sc in previous round (= 12 sc).

Round 3: *sc 1 in next st, then inc 1 in next st*, repeat 5 more times from * to * (= 18 sc).

Round 4: *sc 2, inc 1*, repeat 5 more times from * to * (= 24 sc).

Round 5: *sc 3, inc 1*, repeat 5 more times from * to * (= 30 sc).

Rounds 6–12: sc 1 in each of the 30 sc in previous round (= 30 sc).

Finish work with 1 sl st and break yarn (a).

2. Use the grey colorway for the body.

Round 1: ch 2, then add 6 sc in the 1st ch.

Round 2: inc 1 in each sc in previous round (= 12 sc).

Round 3: *sc 1 in next st, then inc 1 in next st*, repeat 5 more times from * to * (= 18 sc).

Round 4: *sc 2, inc 1*, repeat 5 more times from * to * (= 24 sc).

Round 5: *sc 3, inc 1*, repeat 5 more times from * to * (= 30 sc).

Round 6: *sc 4, inc 1*, repeat 5 more times from * to * (= 36 sc).

Rounds 7–15: sc 1 in each of the 36 sc in previous round (= 36 sc).

Round 16: *sc 4, dec 1*, repeat 5 more times from * to * (= 30 sc).

Round 17: sc 1 in each of the 30 sc in previous round (= 30 sc).

Finish work with 1 sl st and break yarn.

Stuff the body of the owl. (a).

3. Use the grey colorway for the wings.

>>

>>

Round 1: ch 2, then add 6 sc in the 1st ch.

Round 2: inc 1 in each sc in previous round (= 12 sc).

Rounds 3-10: sc 1 in each of the 12 sc in previous round (= 12 sc).

Finish work with 1 sl st and break yarn. Make a second identical wing.

Do not stuff the wings (a).

4. Use the white colorway for the eye contours.

Round 1: ch 2, then add 6 sc in the 1st ch.

Round 2: inc 1 in each sc in previous round (= 12 sc).

Round 3: *sc 1 in next st, then inc 1 in next st*, repeat 5 more times from * to * (= 18 sc).

Finish work with 1 sl st and break yarn (b).

Repeat for 2nd eye contour.

5. Use the white colorway for the tummy.

Round 1: ch 2, then add 6 sc in the 1st ch.

Round 2: inc 1 in each sc in previous round (= 12 sc).

Round 3: *sc 1 in next st, then inc 1 in next st*, repeat 5 more times from * to * (= 18 sc).

Round 4: *sc 2, inc 1*, repeat 5 more times from * to * (= 24 sc).

Finish work with 1 sl st and break yarn (b).

Stuff.

NOTE: *When breaking the yarn, make sure to leave a tail approximately 20 cm (8") long. This will be used to join together the various parts of the owl's body.*

Assembly

6. Begin by attaching the eyes to the head (see **Creating the Face**, page 11). Simultaneously insert the black post into the center of the eye contour and into the head between rounds 9 and 10 (c). Next, clip the white disc onto the black post by pressing forcefully. Repeat this process for the second eye. The two white eye contours should touch each other.

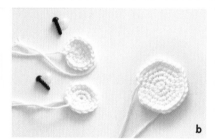
b

c

d

e

7. Use the white sewing thread to attach the eye contours to the head with a running stitch (d).

8. Use the red sewing thread and a regular sewing needle to embroider a beak onto the owl. This is achieved by sewing increasingly small back and forth stitches to make a beak shape (e).

9. Next, join the owl's head and body using a tapestry needle. Stuff the head as you work (f).

10. Sew the wings along the seam line connecting the owl's head and body (g).

11. If desired, embroider the owl's tummy with running stitches using a sewing needle and red thread (h).

12. Use the tapestry needle to sew the tummy onto the body (i).

Your owl is now completed.

NOTE: *When cutting thread or yarn after joining two pieces together, make sure you leave a tail long enough to be hidden inside the owl's body.*

Variation

For an owl approximately 20 cm (8") high, suitable as a baby gift or similar, simply double the yarn and use a 6.0 mm hook. If this toy is destined for a child age 3 or under, it is safer to embroider the eyes rather than using plastic ones.

f

g

h

i

• HAPPY VILLAGE •

I have chosen to present this set of little houses as a decorative feature. However, you could just as easily use them as teapot trivets, or perhaps as cuddly pillows. Simply increase the initial number of chain stitches and stuff them thoroughly.

DIFFICULTY LEVEL: ★ — DIMENSIONS OF BLUE HOUSE: 24 X 13 CM (9.5" X 5")

★ Materials

For one house:

1 ball size 3 pale blue cotton crochet thread
1 ball size 3 grey cotton crochet thread
1 ball size 3 pale pink cotton crochet thread
1 ball size 3 silver metallic crochet thread
Black sewing thread
1 crochet hook – 6.0 mm
1 crochet hook – 3.0 mm
Scraps of black felt
Basic kit (see page 5)

★ Stitches

Chain stitch (ch)
Single crochet stitch (sc)
Slip stitch (sl st)

Instructions

1. To make the walls of the house, use doubled pale blue yarn and the 6.0 mm hook. The base of the house is worked in the round for the initial stitches. Make a chain of 23 ch, then 1 ch to turn (a).

Round 1: sc 1 in each of the first 22 sc in the chain, and sc 3 in the 23rd ch, or the very 1st ch in the chain [diagram below and (b)]. On the return round, sc 1 in each of the next 22 ch and finish with sc 3 in the ch used to turn. You have now finished the 1st round (= 50 sc) (c).

Rounds 2-23: sc 1 in each of the 50 sc in previous round (= 50 sc). Don't be surprised if your work looks somewhat warped in the beginning (d). The walls will begin to look more rectangular by the 5th round (e, f).

2. To make the roof (triangle), use the grey colorway doubled with the silver thread on the size 6 hook. Work in back-and-forth crochet.

Row 1: ch 2, then sc 2 in the 1st ch, ch 1, then turn (= 2 sc).

Row 2: sc 1, inc 1 in the next st, ch 1, then turn (= 3 sc).

Row 3: sc 2, inc 1 in the next st, ch 1, then turn (= 4 sc).

Row 4: sc 3, inc 1 in the next st, ch 1, then turn (= 5 sc).

× **Single crochet**
◯ **Chain stitch**

a

b

c

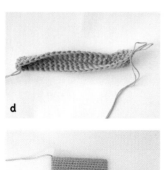

Row 5: sc 4, inc 1 in the next st, ch 1 and turn (= 6 sc).

Row 6: sc 5, inc 1 in the next st, ch 1 and turn (= 7 sc).

Rows 7-26: sc 1 in each sc in previous row, inc 1 at the end of every row and ch 1 to turn. Repeat this sequence to the end of the triangle.

Finish work with 1 sl st and break yarn (g).

Make a second identical triangle for the back side of the roof.

3. To make the door, use the pale pink colorway. Using a size 3 hook, ch 10, then ch 1. Crochet in back-and-forth on this chain. End each row with ch 1 to obtain the height of the 1st sc, then turn.

Row 1: sc 1 in each ch in the chain.

Rows 2-14: sc 1 in each of the 10 sc in previous row (= 10 sc). If you wish to add a border, add sc around the entire door.

Finish work with 1 sl st and break yarn.

Assembly

4. Begin by joining the two roof sections, right sides together.

5. Cut small triangles from the black felt scraps, then gather together all pieces for assembly (h). Sew the roof and walls. Create the bunting by sewing on the felt triangles with tiny stitches using black sewing thread (h).

Variation
You may also wish to create houses in varying sizes to form a little village. Simply alter the number of stitches in the initial chain and increase the number of rows to obtain the desired height of the house. The felt bunting can be replaced by crocheted flags. To do so, follow the roof instructions until the 5th row.

Variation
This pattern can also be used to make a pillow. To do so, increase the number of chain stitches in the initial chain, and thoroughly stuff the house during assembly.

• MARIETTE •

I am fairly sure you have never met this migratory bird, with her pretty golden wings and black feet. Mariette is a rather unusual-looking creature, so anything goes when it comes to making this cuddly favorite!

DIFFICULTY LEVEL: ★ — DIMENSIONS: 29 X 11 CM (11.5" X 4.25")

★ Materials
1 ball size 3 white cotton crochet thread
1 ball size 3 tan cotton crochet thread
1 ball size 3 black cotton crochet thread
1 skein of pink pearl cotton floss
1 ball size 3 gold metallic crochet thread
1 crochet hook – 3.0 mm
2 plastic safety eyes, black and brown, 6 mm
Basic kit (see page 5)

★ Stitches
Chain stitch (ch)
Single crochet stitch (sc)
Slip stitch (sl st)
Double crochet (dc)

Instructions

1. Use the white colorway for the head and body, from rounds 1-20. From rounds 21-55, use the tan colorway doubled with the gold thread. Return to the white colorway from round 56 to the end.

Round 1: ch 2, then add 6 sc in the 1st ch.

Round 2: inc 1 in each sc in previous round (= 12 sc).

Round 3: *sc 1 in next st, then inc 1 in next st*, repeat 5 more times from * to * (= 18 sc).

Round 4: *sc 2, inc 1*, repeat 5 more times from * to * (= 24 sc).

Round 5: *sc 3, inc 1*, repeat 5 more times from * to * (= 30 sc).

Round 6: *sc 4, inc 1*, repeat 5 more times from * to * (= 36 sc).

Round 7: *sc 5, inc 1*, repeat 5 more times from * to * (= 42 sc).

Round 8: *sc 6, inc 1*, repeat 5 more times from * to * (= 48 sc).

Round 9: *sc 7, inc 1*, repeat 5 more times from * to * (= 54 sc).

Rounds 10-14: sc 1 in each of the 54 sc in previous round (= 54 sc).

Round 15: *sc 7, dec 1*, repeat 5 more times from * to * (= 48 sc).

Round 16: sc 1 in each of the 48 sc in previous round (= 48 sc).

Round 17: *sc 6, dec 1*, repeat 5 more times from * to * (= 42 sc).

Round 18: sc 1 in each of the 42 sc in previous round (= 42 sc).

Round 19: *sc 5, dec 1*, repeat 5 more times from * to * (= 36 sc).

Round 20: sc 1 in each of the 36 sc in previous round (= 36 sc). Break yarn.

Round 21: using the tan colorway doubled with the gold thread, *sc 4, dec 1*, repeat 5 more times from * to * (= 30 sc).

Clip in the plastic safety eyes between the 10th and 11th rounds. Leave a space roughly 11 sc wide between the two eyes (see **Creating the Face**, page 11).

>>

>>

Round 22: *sc 3, dec 1*, repeat 5 more times from * to * (= 24 sc). Stuff the head.

Rounds 23-32: sc 1 in each of the 24 sc in previous round (= 24 sc).

Round 33: *sc 3, inc 1*, repeat 5 more times from * to * (= 30 sc).

Round 34: sc 1 in each of the 30 sc in previous round (= 30 sc).

Round 35: *sc 4, inc 1*, repeat 5 more times from * to * (= 36 sc).

Round 36: sc 1 in each of the 36 sc in previous round (= 36 sc).

Round 37: *sc 5, inc 1*, repeat 5 more times from * to * (= 42 sc).

Round 38: *sc 6, inc 1*, repeat 5 more times from * to * (= 48 sc).

Round 39: *sc 7, inc 1*, repeat 5 more times from * to * (= 54 sc) (a).

Rounds 40-55: sc 1 in each of the 54 sc in previous round (= 54 sc). Break yarn.

Round 56: using the white colorway, *sc 7, dec 1*, repeat 5 more times from * to * (= 48 sc). Stuff the body.

Round 57: *sc 6, dec 1*, repeat 5 more times from * to * (= 42 sc).

Round 58: *sc 5, dec 1*, repeat 5 more times from * to * (= 36 sc).

Round 59: *sc 4, dec 1*, repeat 5

a

more times from * to * (= 30 sc). Finish stuffing the body.

Round 60: *sc 3, dec 1*, repeat 5 more times from * to * (= 24 sc).

Round 61: *sc 2, dec 1*, repeat 5 more times from * to * (= 18 sc).

Round 62: *sc 1, dec 1*, repeat 5 more times from * to * (= 12 sc).

Round 63: dec 6 (= 6 sc).

Round 64: dec 3 to close the lower body. Finish with 1 sl st and break yarn.

2. Use the white colorway for the wings.

Round 1: ch 2, then add 6 sc in the 1st ch.

Round 2: sc 1 in each of the 6 sc in previous round (= 6 sc).

Round 3: inc 1 in each sc in previous round (= 12 sc).

Round 4: sc 1 in each of the 12 sc in previous round (= 12 sc).

Round 5: *sc 1, inc 1*, repeat 5 more times from * to * (= 18 sc).

Rounds 6-9: sc 1 in each of the 18 sc in previous round (= 18 sc).

>>

\>\>

Round 10: *sc 3, dec1*, repeat 2 more times from * to *, end round with sc 1, dec 1 (= 14 sc).

Rounds 11-12: sc 1 in each of the 14 sc in previous round (= 14 sc).

Round 13: *sc 1, dec 1*, repeat 3 more times from * to *, end round with sc 2 (= 10 sc).

Round 14: sc 1 in each of the 10 sc in previous round (= 10 sc). Finish with 1 sl st and break yarn.

Make a second identical wing. Do not stuff wings.

3. Use the black colorway for the legs.

Round 1: ch 2, then add 6 sc in the 1st ch.

Rounds 2-19: sc 1 in each of the 6 sc in previous round (= 6 sc).

Flatten the tops of the legs. Sc 3, dc 1, taking care to insert hook into the 2 facing stitches. This will close the tube formed by the leg (b). Dc 3 into the next st and end with dc 2 in the last st. Finish with 1 sl st and break yarn. Make a second identical leg (c). Do not stuff legs.

4. To make the beak, use the black colorway doubled with the pink pearl cotton thread.

Round 1: ch 2, then add 6 sc in the 1st ch.

Rounds 2-7: sc 1 in each of the 6 sc in previous round (= 6 sc). Finish with 1 sl st and break yarn. Stuff the beak (d).

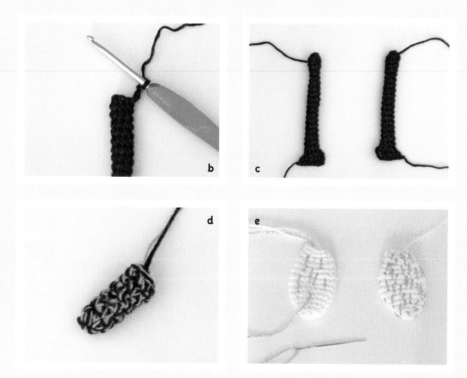

Assembly

5. Begin by embroidering the wings with the gold thread (e). Gather together all pieces for assembly (f), then sew the wings on either side of the bird's body, at the height of round 35.

6. Next, sew the beak at the height of round 12. Using a double knot, attach a few strands of thread to the stitching on either side of the head, at the height of round 6.

7. Sew the legs under the bird's torso. Using a wool needle, embroider a few feathers onto the body.

8. Color in the cheeks (see **Creating the Face** on page 11).

Variation
How about inserting some tiny bells inside the body to make a musical toy?

• SUSHI PLATTER! •

Fill your kids' sushi plate! Dig into egg, salmon, shrimp, tuna, sea bass sushi … unless avocado, cucumber and salmon, and crab maki are more to your taste. All you need to do is switch up the thread colors while following the basic directions. There's something to satisfy even the fussiest customer.

DIFFICULTY LEVEL: ★ — DIMENSIONS OF ONE PIECE OF SUSHI: 6 X 3.5 CM (2.25" X 1.5")

★ **Materials**

1 ball size 3 ivory cotton crochet thread
1 ball size 3 black cotton crochet thread
1 ball size 3 crimson cotton crochet thread
1 ball size 3 orange cotton crochet thread
1 ball size 3 white cotton crochet thread
1 ball size 3 light green cotton crochet thread
1 skein of white pearl cotton floss
1 crochet hook – 3.0 mm
Basic kit (see page 5)

★ **Stitches**

Chain stitch (ch)
Single crochet stitch (sc)
Slip stitch (sl st)
Double crochet (dc)
Double treble (dtr)

To make the sushi

1. Use the ivory colorway to make the rice layer.

Round 1: ch 2, then sc 8 in the 1st ch.

Round 2: inc 1 in each sc in previous round (= 16 sc).

Round 3: *sc 1 in next st, then inc 1 in next st*, repeat 7 more times from * to * (= 24 sc).

Rounds 4-15: sc 1 in each of 24 sc in previous round (= 24 sc).

Round 16: *sc 1 in next st, then dec 1 in next st*, repeat 7 more times from * to * (= 16 sc). Stuff the layer of rice.

Round 17: dec 1 in each sc (= 8 sc).

Round 18: dec until layer of rice is closed. Finish and break yarn (see a, left).

2. Use the crimson colorway to make the fish slice. Using the color of your choice, ch 10. Crochet back-and-forth, starting each row with 1 ch up to the height of the 1st sc.

Row 1: sc 1 in each ch.

Rows 2-12: (+/- depending on the actual length once the layer of rice has been stuffed): sc 1 in each of the 10 sc in the previous row (= 10 sc). Finish and break yarn (see a, left).

3. Make the black seaweed ring surrounding the sushi. Depending on actual size of the sushi when stuffed, ch ~30 with black thread. Sl st 1 in 1st ch to create a ring. Finish and break yarn.

4. Working back-and-forth, use the orange colorway, doubled with white pearl cotton, to make the shrimp.

Row 1: ch 3, then ch 1 to turn.

Row 2: inc 1, sc 1, inc 1, ch 1 (= 5 sc).

Row 3: inc 1, sc 3, inc 1, ch 1 (= 7 sc).

Row 4: inc 1, sc 5, inc 1, ch 1 (= 9 sc).

Rows 5-8: sc 1 in each of the 9 sc in previous row, then ch 1 (= 9 sc)

>>

a

>>

Row 9: dec 1, sc 5, dec 1, ch 1 (= 7 sc).

Row 10: sc 1 in each of the 7 sc in previous row, then ch 1 (= 7 sc).

Row 11: dec 1, sc 3, dec 1, ch 1 (= 5 sc).

Row 12: sc 1 in each of the 5 sc in previous row, then ch 1 (= 5 sc).

Row 13: dec 1, sc 1, dec 1, ch 1 (= 3 sc).

From this point, do not break the yarn, but rather, ch 4, then ch 1 to turn. Sc 1 in the 1st ch on the hook, dc 1 in 2nd ch, dtr 1 in 3rd ch, dtr 1 in 4th ch. Sl st in 2nd sc in row 13. At this point, continue by once again adding ch 4 to turn, and then make a 2nd identical part of the tail. Finish with 1 sl st in the 3rd sc in row 13. Finish and break yarn (b).

5. If desired, use the white colorway to embroider lines on top of the fish slice (b). Assemble the fish sushi by sewing the top of the sushi onto the rice layer, stitch to stitch, using a wool needle (d). Do the same with the shrimp sushi (e). Place the black seaweed ring around the sushi (f). Weave the ends into the piece of sushi.

To make the maki

6. Use the black or ivory colorways to make the sheet of rice or the nori. Make a 24 ch chain. Close it in a ring shape with 1 sl st in the 1st ch in the chain.

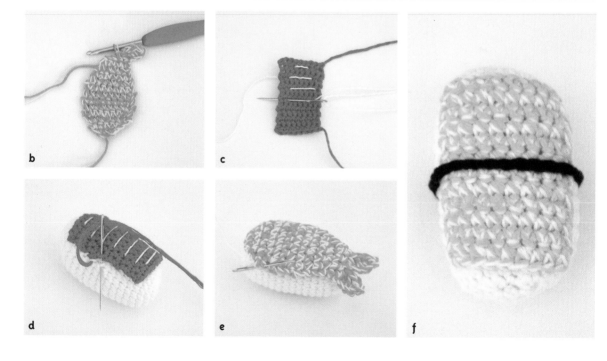

Round 1: sc 1 in each ch in the chain (= 24 sc).

Rounds 2-6: sc 1 in each sc in previous round (= 24 sc). Finish with 1 sl st and break yarn (g).

7. Make the garnish for the maki.

Round 1: with crimson colorway, ch 2, then add 6 sc in the 1st ch.

Round 2: inc 1 in each sc in previous round (= 12 sc).

Round 3: with pale green colorway, *sc 1 in next st, inc 1 in next st*, repeat 5 more times from * to * (= 18 sc).

Round 4: with ivory colorway, *sc 2, inc 1*, repeat 5 more times from

* to * (= 24 sc). Finish with 1 sl st and break yarn (g). Make a second identical garnish (h).

8. Assemble the maki roll by sewing the two garnishes above and below the sheet of rice or the nori, using a tapestry needle. Stuff the maki roll as you go. Make sure to weave in all yarn ends (i, j).

TIP: *If you choose to make the nori sheet, use an ultra-thin sewing needle and very fine sewing thread during assembly, so the stitches are less visible.*

Variation

To make maki and sashimi of various flavors, simply change thread color. To give the sushi elements a mottled, heathery look, use the main color thread doubled with very fine white pearl cotton floss. Continue to work these threads on a 3.0 mm hook.

• PIRUM PARUM •

I have long admired the work of illustrator Élisabeth Dunker. Like many, I instantly fell in love with her famous character, Pirum Parum. Many thanks to Élisabeth Dunker, who graciously gave me permission to reproduce this adorable pear with its expressive face.

DIFFICULTY LEVEL: ★ — DIMENSIONS: 16 X 10 CM (6.25" X 4")

★ Materials

1 ball size 3 grey cotton crochet thread
1 ball size 3 pale pink cotton crochet thread
1 ball size 3 brown cotton crochet thread
1 skein of pink pearl cotton floss
Black embroidery thread
Pink sewing thread
Crochet hooks – 6.0 mm, 3.0 mm, and 1.5 mm
2 plastic safety eyes, black, 6 mm
Basic kit (see page 5)

★ Stitches

Chain stitch (ch)
Single crochet stitch (sc)
Slip stitch (sl st)
Double crochet (dc)
Double treble (dtr)

Instructions

1. Use the grey colorway to make the body of the pear.

Round 1: using the 6.0 mm hook and doubled thread, ch 2, then add 6 sc in the 1st ch.

Round 2: inc 1 in each sc in previous round (= 12 sc).

Round 3: *sc 1 in next st, inc 1 in next st*, repeat 5 more times from * to * (= 18 sc).

Rounds 4-5: sc 1 in each sc in previous round (= 18 sc).

Round 6: *sc 1, inc 1*, repeat 5 more times from * to * (= 24 sc).

Rounds 7-10: sc 1 in each of 24 sc in previous round (= 24 sc).

Round 11: *sc 3, inc 1*, repeat 5 more times from * to * (= 30 sc).

Rounds 12-16: sc 1 in each of 30 sc in previous round (= 30 sc).

Round 17: *sc 4, inc 1*, repeat 5 more times from * to * (= 36 sc).

Round 18: *sc 5, inc 1*, repeat 5 more times from * to * (= 42 sc).

Round 19: *sc 6, inc 1*, repeat 5 more times from * to * (= 48 sc).

Round 20: *sc 7, inc 1*, repeat 5 more times from * to * (= 54 sc).

Rounds 21-26: sc 1 in each of 54 sc in previous round (= 54 sc).

Round 27: *sc 7, dec 1*, repeat 5 more times from * to * (= 48 sc).

Round 28: *sc 6, dec 1*, repeat 5 more times from * to * (= 42 sc).

Round 29: *sc 5, dec 1*, repeat 5 more times from * to * (= 36 sc).

Round 30: *sc 4, dec 1*, repeat 5 more times from * to * (= 30 sc). Begin stuffing the pear and clip in the plastic safety eyes between rounds 20 and 21, leaving a 9 sc space (roughly 6 cm / 2.25") space between them (see **Creating the Face**, page 11).

>>

a

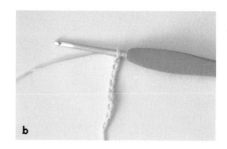
b

c

d

>>

Round 31: *sc 3, dec 1*, repeat 5 more times from * to * (= 24 sc).

Round 32: *sc 2, dec 1*, repeat 5 more times from * to * (= 18 sc). Finish stuffing tightly.

Round 33: *sc 1, dec 1*, repeat 5 more times from * to * (= 12 sc).

Round 34: dec 6 (= 6 sc).

Round 35: dec 3 to close the head. Finish with 1 sl st and break yarn, leaving a 70 cm (27.5") tail to give the pear its curved shape (a).

2. Use the pink pearl cotton and the 1.5 mm hook to make the cheeks.

Round 1: ch 2, then add 6 sc in the 1st ch.

Round 2: inc 1 in each sc in previous round (= 12 sc).

Round 3: *sc 1 in next st, inc 1 in next st*, repeat 5 more times from * to * (= 18 sc).

Finish with 1 sl st and break yarn. Make a second identical cheek.

3. Use the pale pink colorway and the 3.0 mm hook to make the leaf. Ch 10 (b).

Round 1: ch 1 to turn, sc 1, dc 1, dtr 6, dc 1, sc 3 in the same stitch (c), dc 1, dtr 6, dc 1, sc 1. Finish with 1 sl st and break yarn (d).

4. Use the brown colorway and the 3.0 mm hook to make the stem. Make a chain by ch 9, then ch 1 to turn (e).

Turn your work over and sc 1 in each of the 9 ch in the previous round (f). Finish with 1 sl st and break yarn.

Assembly

5. Using a large doll needle, run the tail back and forth through the pear, then pull until the desired shape is achieved. Weave the yarn end into the pear's body.

6. Using pink sewing thread and a regular sewing needle, sew one cheek below each eye. Embroider the nose with black embroidery thread (g).

7. Next, sew the stem and leaf to the top of the pear (h).

Variation

Using a 3.0 mm hook and a single strand of green or yellow yarn, you can start or complete a basketful of fruit. They will be nearly half the size of Pirum Parum (9 cm / 3.5") but will be equally delicious!

• BRUSSELS •

My daughter, Louise, has fallen in love with this little character. With her flattened shape and droopy ears, Brussels can safely hide anywhere, without worrying about the cat finding her...

DIFFICULTY LEVEL: ★ ★ — DIMENSIONS: 22 X 9 CM (8.7" X 3.5")

★ Materials

1 ball size 3 cream cotton crochet thread
1 ball size 3 chartreuse cotton crochet thread
1 ball size 3 gold metallic thread
Brown embroidery thread
Crochet hook – 3.0 mm
Plastic safety nose and eyes, black, 6 mm
Strip of 2 x 30 cm (0.75" x 11.75") floral print fabric
Basic kit (see page 5)

★ Stitches

Chain stitch (ch)
Single crochet stitch (sc)
Slip stitch (sl st)

a

Instructions

1. Use the cream colorway to make the head.

Round 1: ch 2, then add 6 sc in the 1st ch.

Round 2: inc 1 in each sc in previous round (= 12 sc).

Round 3: *sc 1 in next st, then inc 1 in next st*, repeat 5 more times from * to * (= 18 sc).

Round 4: *sc 2, inc 1*, repeat 5 more times from * to * (= 24 sc).

Round 5: *sc 3, inc 1*, repeat 5 more times from * to * (= 30 sc).

Round 6: *sc 4, inc 1*, repeat 5 more times from * to * (= 36 sc).

Round 7: *sc 5, inc 1*, repeat 5 more times from * to * (= 42 sc).

Round 8: *sc 6, inc 1*, repeat 5 more times from * to * (= 48 sc).

Rounds 9-22: sc 1 in each of the 48 sc in previous round (= 48 sc). Finish with 1 sl st and break yarn.

2. Use the cream colorway to make the legs. Work rounds 7, 8, 12, and 13 with the chartreuse colorway doubled with the gold thread.

Round 1: ch 2, then add 6 sc in the 1st ch.

Round 2: inc 1 in each sc in previous round (= 12 sc).

Round 3: *sc 1 in next st, inc 1 in next st*, repeat 5 more times from * to * (= 18 sc).

Rounds 4-15: sc 1 in each of the 18 sc in previous round (= 18 sc). Finish with 1 sl st and break yarn. Make a second identical leg, but do not break yarn.

3. Use the cream colorway to make the torso. Work rounds 2, 3, 8, and 9 with the chartreuse colorway doubled with the gold thread.

Round 1: ch 7 at the end of the 1st leg (a), then sc 1 in each of the 18 sc of the 2nd leg, then ch 7, sc 1 in each of the 18 sc of the 1st leg (this gives us 7 + 18 + 7 + 18 = 50).

>>

>>

Rounds 2-25: sc 1 in each of the 50 sc in previous round (= 50 sc) (b, c).

Round 26: sc 23, dec 1, sc 23, dec 1 (= 48 sc). Finish with 1 sl st and break yarn. Close the opening at the crotch using cotton or sewing thread. Stuff the legs and torso.

4. Use the cream colorway to make the arms.

Round 1: ch 2, then add 6 sc in the 1st ch.

Round 2: inc 1 in each sc in previous round (= 12 sc).

Rounds 3-23: sc 1 in each of the 12 sc in previous round (= 12 sc).

Finish with 1 sl st and break yarn. Make a second identical arm. Do not stuff arms.

5. Use the cream colorway to make the ears.

Round 1: ch 2, then add 6 sc in the 1st ch.

Round 2: sc 1 in each of the 6 sc in previous round (= 6 sc).

Round 3: inc 1 in each sc in previous round (= 12 sc).

Rounds 4-5: sc 1 in each of the 12 sc in previous round (= 12 sc).

Round 6: *sc 1 in next st, inc 1 in next st*, repeat 5 more times from * to * (= 18 sc).

Round 7: sc 1 in each of the 18 sc in previous round (= 18 sc).

Round 8: *sc 2, inc 1*, repeat 5 more times from * to * (= 24 sc).

Round 9: sc 1 in each of the 24 sc in previous round (= 24 sc).

Round 10: *sc 3, inc 1*, repeat 5 more times from * to * (= 30 sc).

Rounds 11-14: sc 1 in each of the 30 sc in previous round (= 30 sc).

Round 15: *sc 3, dec 1*, repeat 5 more times from * to * (= 24 sc).

Round 16: sc 1 in each of the 24 sc in previous round (= 24 sc).

Round 17: *sc 2, dec 1*, repeat 5 more times from * to * (= 18 sc).

Round 18: sc 1 in each of the 18 sc in previous round (= 18 sc).

Round 19: *sc 1, dec 1*, repeat 5 more times from * to * (= 12 sc).

Round 20: *sc 1, dec 1*, repeat 3 more times from * to * (= 8 sc).

Finish with 1 sl st and break yarn. Make a second identical ear. Do not stuff ears.

b

c

TIP: *As the stripes on this pattern are quite slim, do not break yarn at each color change. Instead, let the unused color run along the inside of Brussels's legs and body.*

Assembly

6. Begin by clipping the nose onto the head at the height of the 13th round, and the eyes at the height of the 12th round. Leave approximately 3 cm (1.25") between each eye and the nose (see **Creating the Face**, page 11).

7. Gather together all pieces for assembly (d). Sew the head and body together using a tapestry needle. Stuff the head and body as you sew. Color in the cheeks (see **Creating the Face**, page 11) (d, e).

8. Using the gold thread, embroider fine lines onto the ears (f). Sew the ears at the height of the 6th round of the head (d).

9. Sew the arms at the height of the penultimate round of the torso.

10. Using brown embroidery thread, embroider claws on the ends of the character's arms and legs. Cut a strip of floral fabric (2 x 30 cm / 0.75" x 11.75") to make a small scarf.

TIP: *Leaving the character's arms and ears unstuffed will make him softer and cuddlier.*

Variation
Brussels would look equally handsome with a crocheted bowtie. To create this look, consult the instructions for the bowtie in the **Josephine** pattern (page 44).

• MINI-TRIO •

Just slip these pocket-sized cuddly toys into their fabric carry bags and they can follow their little owners everywhere. All three character bodies can be created using these instructions – it's up to you to choose the ears and faces for maximum charm and personality!

DIFFICULTY LEVEL: ★★ — EACH TOY MEASURES 12 X 4 CM (4.75" X 1.5")

★ Materials

1 ball size 3 chartreuse cotton crochet thread
1 ball size 3 pale yellow cotton crochet thread
1 ball size 3 grey cotton crochet thread
Neon pink embroidery thread
Thick black embroidery thread
White embroidery thread
Crochet hook – 3.0 mm
Strip of 1 x 30 cm (0.5" x 11.75") floral print fabric
Scraps of thick white felt
Basic kit (see page 5)

★ Stitches

Chain stitch (ch)
Single crochet stitch (sc)
Slip stitch (sl st)

Instructions

1. Use the colorway of your choice to make the legs.

Round 1: ch 2, then add 6 sc in the 1st ch.

Round 2: inc 1 in each sc in previous round (= 12 sc).

Rounds 3-8: sc 1 in each of the 12 sc in previous round (= 12 sc). Finish with 1 sl st and break yarn.

Make a second identical leg, but do not break yarn (a).

2. Use the same colorway to make the torso.

Round 1: place the 1st leg next to the 2nd leg to bring them together. From the 2nd leg, insert the hook into the 1st stitch of the 1st leg (b) and sc 1 in each of the 12 sc, then sc 1 in each of the 12 sc in 2nd leg (this gives us 12 + 12 = 24 sc).

Rounds 2-5: sc 1 in each of the 24 sc in previous round (= 24 sc).

Round 6: sc 5, dec 1, sc 10, dec 1, sc 5 (= 22 sc).

Round 7: sc 1 in each of the 22 sc in previous round (= 22 sc).

Round 8: sc 5, dec 1, sc 10, dec 1, sc 3 (= 20 sc).

Rounds 9-13: sc 1 in each of the 20 sc in previous round (= 20 sc).

Round 14: sc 6, dec 1, sc 12 (= 19 sc).

Round 15: sc 6, dec 1, sc 11 (= 18 sc). Finish with 1 sl st and break yarn.

Stuff thoroughly. Embroider fine lines on the torso with the neon pink thread (c).

>>

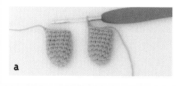

a

b

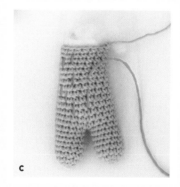

c

>>

3. Use the same colorway to make the head.

Round 1: ch 2, then add 6 sc in the 1st ch.

Round 2: inc 1 in each sc in previous round (= 12 sc).

Round 3: *sc 1 in next st, then inc 1 in next st*, repeat 5 more times from * to * (= 18 sc).

Rounds 4-5: sc 1 in each of the 18 sc in previous round (= 18 sc).

Round 6: *sc 2, inc 1*, repeat 5 more times from * to * (= 24 sc).

Rounds 7-12: sc 1 in each of the 24 sc in previous round (= 24 sc).

Round 13: *sc 2, dec 1*, repeat 5 more times from * to * (= 18 sc). Finish with 1 sl st and break yarn (d).

4. Make one set of ears using the grey colorway.

Round 1: ch 2, then add 6 sc in the 1st ch.

Round 2: *sc 1, inc 1*, repeat 2 more times from * to * (= 9 sc).

Rounds 3-10: sc 1 in each of the 9 sc in previous round (= 9 sc). Finish with 1 sl st and break yarn.

Make a second, identical ear. Do not stuff (e).

5. Make one set of ears using the chartreuse colorway.

Round 1: ch 2, then add 6 sc in the 1st ch.

Round 2: inc 1 in each sc in previous round (= 12 sc).

Round 3: *sc 1 in next st, inc 1 in next st*, repeat 5 more times from * to * (= 18 sc). Finish with 1 sl st and break yarn. Make a second, identical ear. Do not stuff (f).

6. Make one set of ears using the pale yellow colorway.

Round 1: ch 2, then add 6 sc in the 1st ch.

Round 2: sc 1 in each of the 6 sc in previous round (= 6 sc).

Round 3: *sc 1, inc 1*, repeat 2 more times from * to *(= 9 sc).

Rounds 4-5: sc 1 in each of the 9 sc in previous round (= 9 sc). Finish with 1 sl st and break yarn.

Make a second, identical ear. Do not stuff (g).

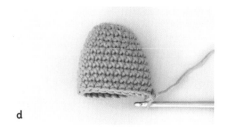

d

e

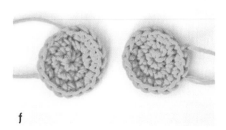

f

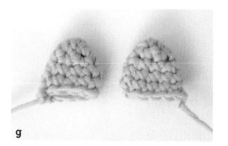

g

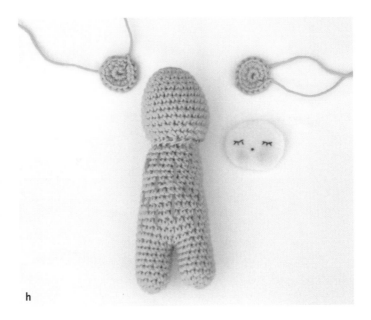

h

Assembly

7. Gather together all pieces for assembly (h). Join the head, torso, and ears of each mini-toy. Thoroughly stuff the head while attaching it to the torso.

8. From the white felt, cut out an oval proportionate with the toy's face. Embroider any desired facial features using a sewing needle and thick black thread. Color in the cheeks (see **Creating the Face**, page 11). Using a regular needle and white sewing thread, sew the face onto the toy's head with small running stitches.

9. Make two more characters to complete the trio. The instructions for the torso and head are identical for all three mini-toys; only the instructions for the ears are different. Feel free to accessorize each toy with a tiny floral fabric scarf (1 x 20 cm / 0.5" x 8") or a crocheted bowtie (see **Josephine** pattern on page 44) made with a basic ch 10 chain.

Variation

If you want a bigger toy, follow the same instructions, but double the yarn and use a 6.0 mm hook.

• JOSEPHINE •

Despite her simple features, Josephine is a most elegant and expressive lady rabbit, with her little grey dress, delicate bonnet, and jaunty bowtie. Josephine's slightly modern, trendy look has made her an all-time favorite with my oldest daughter, six-year-old Lisenn.

DIFFICULTY LEVEL: ★★ — DIMENSIONS: 33 X 9 CM (13" X 3.5")

★ Materials
1 ball size 3 white cotton crochet thread
1 ball size 3 grey cotton crochet thread
1 ball size 3 silver metallic thread
Dark purple embroidery thread
1 crochet hook – 3.0 mm
2 plastic safety eyes, black, 6 mm
Basic kit (see page 5)

★ Stitches
Chain stitch (ch)
Single crochet stitch (sc)
Slip stitch (sl st)

Instructions

1. Use the white colorway to make the head.

Round 1: ch 2, then add 6 sc in the 1st ch.

Round 2: inc 1 in each sc in previous round (= 12 sc).

Round 3: *sc 1 in next st, inc 1 in next st*, repeat 5 more times from * to * (= 18 sc).

Round 4: *sc 2, inc 1*, repeat 5 more times from * to * (= 24 sc).

Round 5: *sc 3, inc 1*, repeat 5 more times from * to * (= 30 sc).

Round 6: *sc 4, inc 1*, repeat 5 more times from * to * (= 36 sc).

Round 7: *sc 5, inc 1*, repeat 5 more times from * to * (= 42 sc).

Round 8: sc 1 in each of the 42 sc in previous round (= 42 sc).

Round 9: *sc 6, inc 1*, repeat 5 more times from * to * (= 48 sc).

Round 10: *sc 7, inc 1*, repeat 5 more times from * to * (= 54 sc).

Rounds 11-17: sc 1 in each of the 54 sc in previous round (= 54 sc).

Round 18: *sc 7, dec 1*, repeat 5 more times from * to * (= 48 sc).

Round 19: *sc 6, dec 1*, repeat 5 more times from * to * (= 42 sc).

Round 20: *sc 5, dec 1*, repeat 5 more times from * to * (= 36 sc).

Round 21: *sc 4, dec 1*, repeat 5 more times from * to * (= 30 sc).

Round 22: *sc 3, dec 1*, repeat 5 more times from * to * (= 24 sc). At the end of this round, clip in the plastic safety eyes between the 13th and 14th rounds, leaving a 4-5 cm (1.5-2") gap between them (see **Creating the Face**, page 11). Begin stuffing the head.

Round 23: *sc 2, dec 1*, repeat 5 more times from * to * (= 18 sc).

Round 24: *sc 1, dec 1*, repeat 5 more times from * to * (= 12 sc). Finish stuffing the head.

Round 25: dec 6 (= 6 sc).

>>

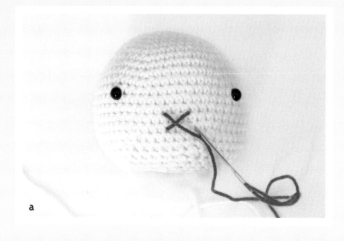

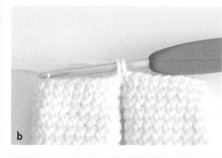

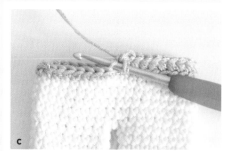

>>

Round 26: dec 3 to close the head. Finish with 1 sl st and break yarn.

Using the purple embroidery thread and a tapestry needle, embroider an X in the middle of the rabbit's head (a).

2. Use the white colorway to make the legs.

Round 1: ch 2, then add 6 sc in the 1st ch.

Round 2: inc 1 in each sc in previous round (= 12 sc).

Round 3: *sc 1 in next st, inc 1 in next st*, repeat 5 more times from * to * (= 18 sc).

Rounds 4-35: sc 1 in each of the 18 sc in previous round (= 18 sc). Finish with 1 sl st and break yarn.

Make a second identical leg. Do not break yarn. Stuff the legs.

3. Use the white colorway to make the torso and, beginning in round 5, the grey colorway, doubled with the

silver thread.

Round 1: place the 1st leg next to the 2nd leg to bring them together. From the 2nd leg, insert the hook into the 1st stitch of the 1st leg (b) and sc 1 in each of the 18 sc of the 1st leg, then sc 1 in each of the 18 sc of the 2nd leg (this gives us 18 + 18 = 36 sc).

Rounds 2-6: sc 1 in each of the 36 sc in previous round (= 36 sc). Use the grey colorway doubled with the silver thread beginning in round 5.

Round 7: sc 1 in each of the 36 sc in previous round, but insert the hook into a strand at the back of the stitch. This will make attaching the skirt onto this row of stitches much easier. (= 36 sc) (c).

Round 8: sc 1 in each of the 36 sc in previous round (= 36 sc).

Round 9: sc 11, dec 1, sc 15, dec 1, sc 6 (= 34 sc).

Rounds 10-12: sc 1 in each of the 34 sc in previous round (= 34 sc).

Round 13: sc 11, dec 1, sc 15, dec 1, sc 4 (= 32 sc).

Rounds 14-21: sc 1 in each of the 32 sc in previous round (= 32 sc).

Round 22: sc 12, dec 1, sc 14, dec 1, sc 2 (= 30 sc). Stuff the torso.

Round 23: sc 1 in each of the 30 sc in previous round (= 30 sc).

Round 24: *sc 3, dec 1*, repeat 5 more times from * to * (= 24 sc).

Rounds 25-26: sc 1 in each of the 24 sc in previous round (= 24 sc).

Round 27: *sc 2, dec 1*, repeat 5 more times from * to * (= 18 sc). Finish stuffing the torso.

Finish with 1 sl st and break yarn.

4. Use the grey colorway doubled with the silver thread to make the skirt.

Round 1: around the middle of the back, insert the hook into a strand at the back of a stitch in the 7th round of the torso. *sc 1, inc 1*, repeat 17 more times from * to * all around the torso (= 54 sc) (d, e).

Rounds 2-8: sc 1 in each of the 54 sc in previous round (= 54 sc). Finish with 1 sl st and break yarn.

5. To make the arms, use the white colorway. Beginning in the 5th round, switch to the grey colorway doubled with the silver thread.

Round 1: ch 2, then add 6 sc in the 1st ch.

Round 2: inc 1 in each sc in previous round (= 12 sc).

Round 3: *sc 2, inc 1*, repeat 3 more times from * to * (= 16 sc).

Rounds 4-5: sc 1 in each of the 16 sc in previous round (= 16 sc). Change color in the 5th round.

Round 6: *sc 3, dec 1*, repeat 2 more times from * to *, and finish the round with sc 1 (= 13 sc).

Rounds 7-29: sc 1 in each of the 13 sc in previous round (= 13 sc). Finish with 1 sl st and break yarn.

Make a second identical arm. Do not stuff the arms.

6. Use the white colorway to make the ears.

Round 1: ch 2, then add 6 sc in the 1st ch.

Round 2: sc 1 in each of the 6 sc in previous round (= 6 sc).

Round 3: inc 1 in each sc in previous round (= 12 sc).

Round 4: sc 1 in each of the 12 sc in previous round (= 12 sc).

Round 5: *sc 1, inc 1*, repeat 5 more times from * to * (= 18 sc).

Rounds 6-9: sc 1 in each of the 18 sc in previous round (= 18 sc).

Round 10: *sc 3, dec 1*, repeat 2 more times from * to *, and finish the round with sc 1, dec 1 (= 14 sc).

Rounds 11-12: sc 1 in each of the 14 sc in previous round (= 14 sc).

>>

d

e

>>

Round 13: *sc 1, dec 1*, repeat 3 more times from * to *, and finish the round with sc 2 (= 10 sc).

Round 14: sc 1 in each of the 10 sc in previous round (= 10 sc). Finish with 1 sl st and break yarn.

Make a second identical ear. Do not stuff the ears.

7. Use the white colorway to make the bonnet.

Round 1: ch 2, then add 6 sc in the 1st ch.

Round 2: inc 1 in each sc in previous round (= 12 sc).

Round 3: *sc 1 in next st, inc 1 in next st*, repeat 5 more times from * to * (= 18 sc).

Round 4: *sc 2, inc 1*, repeat 5 more times from * to * (= 24 sc).

Round 5: *sc 3, inc 1*, repeat 5 more times from * to * (= 30 sc).

Round 6: *sc 4, inc 1*, repeat 5 more times from * to * (= 36 sc).

Round 7: *sc 5, inc 1*, repeat 5 more times from * to * (= 42 sc).

Round 8: *sc 6, inc 1*, repeat 5 more times from * to * (= 48 sc).

Round 9: *sc 7, inc 1*, repeat 5 more times from * to * (= 54 sc).

Rounds 10-13: sc 1 in each of the 54 sc in previous round (= 54 sc).

Row 14: beginning here, work in back-and-forth crochet until the bonnet is completed. Sc 46, then ch 1, then turn the work (= 46 sc).

Row 15: sc 46, ch 1, turn the work (= 46 sc).

Rows 16-18: sc 46, ch 1, turn the work (= 46 sc).

Row 19: this row corresponds to the two openings for the ears. Sc 16, ch 5, skip 5 stitches, sc 4 (after the 5 skipped stitches), ch 5, skip 5 stitches, sc 16, ch 1, turn the work (= 46 sc) (f).

Rows 20-23: sc 46, ch 1, turn the work (= 46 sc). Finish with 1 sl st and break yarn.

8. To make the bowtie, ch 14 in the colorway of your choice. Work in back-and-forth crochet, beginning each row with ch 1 to obtain the height of the 1st sc.

Row 1: sc 1 in each ch of the chain.

Rows 2-12: sc 1 in each of the 14 sc in previous round (= 14 sc). Finish

f

g

h

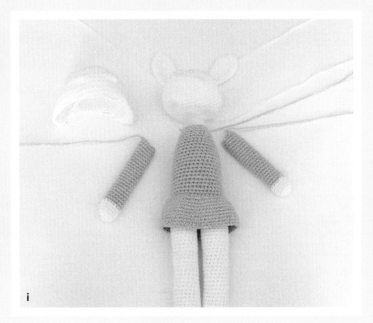

i

with 1 sl st. Break yarn, leaving a tail no less than 40 cm (15.75") long.

Using a tapestry needle, bring the yarn to the center of the crocheted rectangle (g) and roll it around to shape the bowtie. Bring the initial yarn to the center as well, and knot the two together (h).

TIP: *Make sure the head is tightly stuffed. To ensure proper placement, adjust the bonnet on the rabbit's head before joining the head to the body. If the bonnet is too loose, add some extra stuffing into the head and pack it in tightly.*

Variation

You might like to replace the little crocheted bowtie with a pretty floral scarf. Simply cut a strip of fabric approximately 1.5 x 30 cm (0.5" x 11.75").

Assembly

9. Gather together all pieces for assembly (i). Begin by joining the head to the body, stitch for stitch, using a tapestry needle.

10. Next, attach the arms at the height of the penultimate round of the rabbit's body.

11. Sew the ears to the top of the rabbit's head, at the height of the 4th round.

12. Place the bonnet and sew the bowtie onto the neck.

13. Color in the cheeks (see **Creating the Face**, page 11).

• RASPBERRY •

Let yourself fall under the spell of Raspberry's wistful gaze. After much discussion with my children, we still cannot agree on the nature of this character. To some, Raspberry is a lamb; to others, a droopy-eared bunny or perhaps a puppy... the final decision will rest with the owner of this lovable, cuddly toy!

DIFFICULTY LEVEL: ★ ★ — DIMENSIONS: 29 X 11 CM (11.5" X 4.25")

★ Materials

1 ball size 3 white cotton crochet thread
1 ball size 3 tan cotton crochet thread
1 ball size 3 pink cotton crochet thread
Black embroidery thread
1 crochet hook – 3.0 mm
2 plastic safety eyes, black, 6 mm
1.5 x 30 cm (0.5" x 11.75") strip of floral print fabric
Basic kit (see page 5)

★ Stitches

Chain stitch (ch)
Single crochet stitch (sc)
Slip stitch (sl st)

Instructions

1. Use the white colorway to make the head.

Round 1: ch 2, then add 6 sc in the 1st ch.

Round 2: inc 1 in each sc in previous round (= 12 sc).

Round 3: *sc 1 in next st, inc 1 in next st*, repeat 5 more times from * to * (= 18 sc).

Round 4: *sc 2, inc 1*, repeat 5 more times from * to * (= 24 sc).

Round 5: *sc 3, inc 1*, repeat 5 more times from * to * (= 30 sc).

Round 6: *sc 4, inc 1*, repeat 5 more times from * to * (= 36 sc).

Round 7: *sc 5, inc 1*, repeat 5 more times from * to * (= 42 sc).

Round 8: *sc 6, inc 1*, repeat 5 more times from * to * (= 48 sc).

Round 9: sc 1 in each of the 48 sc in previous round (= 48 sc).

Round 10: *sc 7, inc 1*, repeat 5 more times from * to * (= 54 sc).

Rounds 11-17: sc 1 in each of the 54 sc in previous round (= 54 sc).

Round 18: *sc 7, dec 1*, repeat 5 more times from * to * (= 48 sc).

Round 19: sc 1 in each of the 48 sc in previous round (= 48 sc).

Round 20: *sc 6, dec 1*, repeat 5 more times from * to * (= 42 sc). At the end of this round, clip in the plastic safety eyes between the 13th and 14th rounds, leaving a 4-5 cm (1.5"-2") gap between them (see **Creating the Face**, page 11). Begin stuffing.

Round 21: *sc 5, dec 1*, repeat 5 more times from * to * (= 36 sc).

Round 22: *sc 4, dec 1*, repeat 5 more times from * to * (= 30 sc).

Round 23: *sc 3, dec 1*, repeat 5 more times from * to * (= 24 sc). Finish stuffing the head.

Round 24: *sc 2, dec 1*, repeat 5 more times from * to * (= 18 sc). Finish with 1 sl st and break yarn.

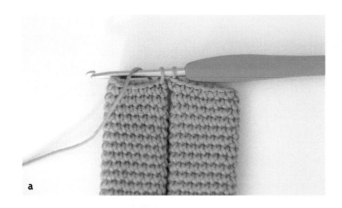

a

>>

2. To make the arms, use the white colorway and, beginning with the 5th round, the pink colorway.

Round 1: ch 2, then add 6 sc in the 1st ch.

Round 2: inc 1 in each sc in previous round (= 12 sc).

Rounds 3-27: sc 1 in each of the 12 sc in previous round (= 12 sc). Change color in the 5th round. Finish with 1 sl st and break yarn.

Make a second identical arm. Do not stuff the arms.

3. To make the legs, use the tan colorway and, beginning with the 6th round, the pink colorway.

Round 1: ch 2, then add 6 sc in the 1st ch.

Round 2: inc 1 in each sc in previous round (= 12 sc).

Round 3: *sc 2, inc 1*, repeat 3 more times from * to * (= 16 sc).

Rounds 4-26: sc 1 in each of the 16 sc in previous round (= 16 sc). Change color in the 6th round. Finish with 1 sl st and break yarn. Make a second identical leg, but do not break yarn.

4. Use the pink colorway to make the torso.

Round 1: place the 1st leg next to the 2nd leg to bring them together. From the 2nd leg, insert the hook into the 1st stitch of the 1st leg (a) and sc 1 in each of the 16 sc of the 1st leg, then sc 1 in each of the 16 sc of the 2nd leg (this gives us 16 + 16 = 32 sc).

Rounds 2-15: sc 1 in each of the 32 sc in previous round (= 32 sc).

Round 16: sc 11, dec 1, sc 14, dec 1, sc 3 (= 30 sc).

Round 17: sc 1 in each of the 30 sc in previous round (= 30 sc).

Round 18: sc 11, dec 1, sc 12, dec 1, sc 3 (= 28 sc). Begin stuffing.

Rounds 19-20: sc 1 in each of the 28 sc in previous round (= 28 sc).

Round 21: sc 11, dec 1, sc 13, dec 1 (= 26 sc).

Round 22: sc 1 in each of the 26 sc in previous round (= 26 sc).

Round 23: sc 11, dec 1, sc 11, dec 1 (= 24 sc).

Rounds 24-25: sc 1 in each of the 24 sc in previous round (= 24 sc).

Round 26: *sc 2, dec 1*, repeat 5 more times from * to * (= 18 sc). Finish stuffing.

Rounds 27-28: sc 1 in each of the 18 sc in previous round (= 18 sc). Finish with 1 sl st and break yarn.

5. Use the pink colorway to make the bonnet.

Round 1: ch 2, then add 6 sc in the 1st ch.

Round 2: inc 1 in each sc in previous round (= 12 sc).

Round 3: *sc 1 in next st, inc 1 in next st*, repeat 5 more times from * to * (= 18 sc).

Round 4: *sc 2, inc 1*, repeat 5 more times from * to * (= 24 sc).

Round 5: *sc 3, inc 1*, repeat 5 more times from * to * (= 30 sc).

Round 6: *sc 4, inc 1*, repeat 5

more times from * to * (= 36 sc).

Round 7: *sc 5, inc 1*, repeat 5 more times from * to * (= 42 sc).

Round 8: *sc 6, inc 1*, repeat 5 more times from * to * (= 48 sc).

Round 9: *sc 7, inc 1*, repeat 5 more times from * to * (= 54 sc).

Round 10: *sc 8, inc 1*, repeat 5 more times from * to * (= 60 sc).

Rounds 11-19: sc 1 in each of the 60 sc in previous round (= 60 sc). Finish with 1 sl st and break yarn.

6. Use the pink colorway to make the ears.

Round 1: ch 2, then add 6 sc in the 1st ch.

Round 2: sc 1 in each of the 6 sc in previous round (= 6 sc).

Round 3: inc 1 in each sc in previous round (= 12 sc).

Round 4: sc 1 in each of the 12 sc in previous round (= 12 sc).

Round 5: *sc 1 in next st, inc 1 in next st*, repeat 5 more times from * to * (= 18 sc).

Round 6: sc 1 in each of the 18 sc in previous round (= 18 sc).

Round 7: *sc 3, inc 1*, repeat 3 more times from * to *. Finish the round with sc 2 (= 22 sc).

Rounds 8-11: sc 1 in each of the 22 sc in previous round (= 22 sc).

Round 12: *sc 3, dec 1*, repeat 3 more times from * to *. Finish the round with sc 2 (= 18 sc).

Round 13: sc 1 in each of the 18 sc in previous round (= 18 sc).

Round 14: *sc 2, dec 1*, repeat 3 more times from * to *. Finish the round with sc 2 (= 14 sc).

Rounds 15-16: sc 1 in each of the 14 sc in previous round (= 14 sc).

Round 17: *sc 1, dec 1*, repeat 3 more times from * to *. Finish the round with sc 2 (= 10 sc).

Rounds 18-19: sc 1 in each of the 10 sc in previous round (= 10 sc). Finish with 1 sl st and break yarn.

Make a second identical ear. Do not stuff the ears.

TIP: Make sure the head is tightly stuffed. To ensure proper placement, adjust the bonnet on Raspberry's head before joining the head to the body. If the bonnet is too loose, add some extra stuffing into the head and pack it in tightly.

Assembly

7. Before joining the various elements, embroider the features on the face and body, as it will be easier to hide the yarn tails. Use black embroidery thread for the nose (b) and white cotton thread for the body (c).

>>

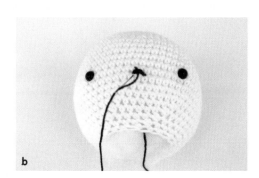

b

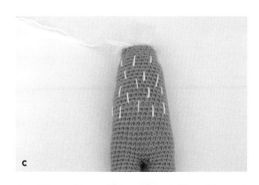

c

>>

8. Gather together all pieces for assembly (d). To begin, sew the head onto the body, stitch for stitch, using a tapestry needle (e).

9. Next, attach the arms at the height of the penultimate round of the body.

10. Sew the ears at the height of the 15th round of the bonnet (f).

11. Color in the cheeks (see **Creating the Face**, page 11).

12. Place the bonnet on Raspberry's head. Cut a small strip (30 x 1.5 cm / 11.75" x 0.5") of floral print fabric for a scarf.

Variation

You can replace the floral scarf with a tulle or crocheted bowtie. In the latter case, complete instructions are provided in the **Josephine** pattern (see page 44).

Variation

You can customize this toy even further by adding stripes over part or all of the body, if desired. To do so, do not break yarn after changing colors. Instead, let the colorway not in use run along the interior of the body of the toy so it is not visible.

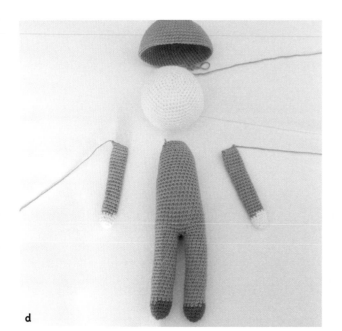

d

e

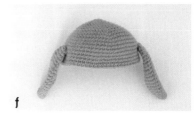

f

• WOLFGANG •

Of course, all of these lovely ladies require a gentleman companion. Who will be the lucky recipient of that beautiful bouquet of red roses? Wolfgang can take his pick! This pattern is based on the same principles as **Josephine** (page 40) and **Raspberry** (page 46).

DIFFICULTY LEVEL: ★ ★ — DIMENSIONS: 30 X 10 CM (11.75" X 4")

★ Materials
1 ball size 3 ivory cotton crochet thread
1 ball size 3 sky blue cotton crochet thread
1 ball size 3 tan cotton crochet thread
1 ball size 3 crimson cotton crochet thread
1 ball white pearl cotton floss
Brown embroidery thread
Black sewing thread
1 crochet hook – 3.0 mm
Scraps of black felt
2 plastic safety eyes, black, 6 mm
Flexible craft wire
Small piece of kraft paper
Basic kit (see page 5)

★ Stitches
Chain stitch (ch)
Single crochet stitch (sc)
Slip stitch (sl st)
Double crochet (dc)

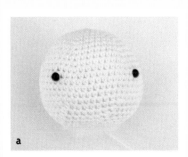

a

Instructions

1. Use the ivory colorway to make the head.

Round 1: ch 2, then add 6 sc in the 1st ch.

Round 2: inc 1 in each sc in previous round (= 12 sc).

Round 3: *sc 1 in next st, inc 1 in next st*, repeat 5 more times from * to * (= 18 sc).

Round 4: *sc 2, inc 1*, repeat 5 more times from * to * (= 24 sc).

Round 5: *sc 3, inc 1*, repeat 5 more times from * to * (= 30 sc).

Round 6: *sc 4, inc 1*, repeat 5 more times from * to * (= 36 sc).

Round 7: *sc 5, inc 1*, repeat 5 more times from * to * (= 42 sc).

Round 8: *sc 6, inc 1*, repeat 5 more times from * to * (= 48 sc).

Round 9: *sc 7, inc 1*, repeat 5 more times from * to * (= 54 sc).

Round 10: sc 1 in each of the 54 sc in previous round (= 54 sc).

Round 11: *sc 8, inc 1*, repeat 5 more times from * to * (= 60 sc).

Rounds 12-19: sc 1 in each of the 60 sc in previous round (= 60 sc). Clip in the plastic safety eyes between the 13th and 14th rounds,

leaving a 14-stitch gap between them (see **Creating the Face**, page 11). Stuff the head tightly (a).

Round 20: *sc 8, dec 1*, repeat 5 more times from * to * (= 54 sc).

Round 21: *sc 7, dec 1*, repeat 5 more times from * to * (= 48 sc).

Round 22: *sc 6, dec 1*, repeat 5 more times from * to * (= 42 sc).

Round 23: *sc 5, dec 1*, repeat 5 more times from * to * (= 36 sc).

Round 24: *sc 4, dec 1*, repeat 5 more times from * to * (= 30 sc).

Round 25: *sc 3, dec 1*, repeat 5 more times from * to * (= 24 sc).

Round 26: *sc 2, dec 1*, repeat 5 more times from * to * (= 18 sc). Finish with 1 sl st and break yarn (a).

>>

2.. To make the legs, use the ivory colorway and, beginning in round 7, the tan colorway.

Round 1: ch 2, then add 6 sc in the 1st ch.

Round 2: inc 1 in each sc in previous round (= 12 sc).

Round 3: *sc 1, inc 1*, repeat 5 more times from * to * (= 18 sc).

Round 4: *sc 2, inc 1*, repeat 5 more times from * to * (= 24 sc).

Rounds 5-35: sc 1 in each of the 24 sc in previous round (= 24 sc). Change color in round 7. Finish with 1 sl st and break yarn.

Make a second identical leg. Do not break yarn. Stuff the legs.

3. To make the torso, use the tan colorway and, beginning in round 5, the sky blue colorway doubled with one strand of white pearl cotton.

Round 1: place the 1st leg next to the 2nd leg to bring them together. From the 2nd leg, insert the hook into the 1st stitch of the 1st leg and sc 1 in each of the 24 sc of the 1st leg, then sc 1 in each of the 24 sc of the 2nd leg (this gives us 24 + 24 = 48 sc).

Round 2: inc 2, sc 24, inc 2, sc 24 (= 52 sc).

Rounds 3-11: sc 1 in each of the 52 sc in previous round (= 52 sc). Note: in round 5, change color and insert the hook only into the stitch's back strand, to create a dividing line between the pants and the sweater (b).

Round 12: dec 1, sc 13, dec 1, sc 21, dec 1, sc 12 (= 49 sc).

Rounds 13-14: sc 1 in each of the 49 sc in previous round (= 49 sc).

Round 15: sc 13, dec 1, sc 21, dec 1, sc 11 (= 47 sc).

Rounds 16-17: sc 1 in each of the 47 sc in previous round (= 47 sc).

Round 18: sc 23, dec 1, sc 20, dec 1 (= 45 sc).

Round 19: sc 1 in each of the 45 sc in previous round (= 45 sc).

Round 20: sc 14, dec 1, sc 18, dec 1, sc 9 (= 43 sc).

Round 21: dec 1, sc 12, dec 1, sc 7, dec 1, sc 7, dec 1, sc 9 (= 39 sc).

Round 22: dec 1, then finish the round with sc 37 (= 38 sc).

Round 23: dec 1, sc 9, dec 1, sc 9, dec 1, sc 9, dec 1, sc 3 (= 34 sc).

Round 24: dec 1, sc 8, dec 1, sc 6, dec 1, sc 6, dec 1, sc 6 (= 30 sc).

Round 25: *sc 3, dec 1*, repeat 5 more times from * to * (= 24 sc). Firmly stuff the torso.

Round 26: *sc 2, dec 1*, repeat 5 more times from * to * (= 18 sc).

Round 27: sc 1 in each of the 18 sc in previous round (= 18 sc). Finish with 1 sl st and break yarn.

4. To make the arms, use the ivory colorway and, beginning in round 6, the sky blue colorway doubled with one strand of white pearl cotton.

Round 1: ch 2, then add 6 sc in the 1st ch.

Round 2: inc 1 in each sc in previous round (= 12 sc).

b

c

d

e

\>\>

Round 3: *sc 2, inc 1*, repeat 3 more times from * to * (= 16 sc).

Rounds 4-30: sc 1 in each of the 16 sc in previous round (= 16 sc). Change color in the 6th round. Finish with 1 sl st and break yarn.

Make a second identical arm. Do not stuff the arms (c).

5. Use the ivory colorway to make the ears.

Round 1: ch 2, then add 6 sc in the 1st ch.

Round 2: sc 1 in each of the 6 sc in previous round (= 6 sc).

Round 3: inc 1 in each sc in previous round (= 12 sc).

Round 4: sc 1 in each of the 12 sc in previous round (= 12 sc).

Round 5: *sc 2, inc 1*, repeat 3 more times from * to * (= 16 sc).

Round 6: sc 1 in each of the 16 sc in previous round (= 16 sc).

Round 7: *sc 3, inc 1*, repeat 3 more times from * to * (= 20 sc).

Round 8: sc 1 in each of the 20 sc in previous round (= 20 sc). Finish with 1 sl st and break yarn.

Make a second identical ear. Do not stuff the ears (d).

Assembly and Finishing

6. Gather together all pieces for assembly (e). To begin, sew the head onto the body using a tapestry needle. Finish tightly stuffing the head and the body as you join the two parts.

7. Next, attach the arms to the torso, at the height of the penultimate round.

8. Sew the ears on top of the head, at the height of the 5th round.

9. Cut out a mustache from the black felt scraps. Sew the mustache in the center of the face, using a sewing needle and fine black thread. Color in the cheeks (see **Creating the Face**, page 11).

10. Work back-and-forth to make a rose, using the crimson colorway.

Row 1: ch 13 then ch 3 to turn.

Row 2: in the 3rd ch from the hook, *dc 6, then sc 1 in the next st* (f),

Variation
Transform this whiskered cat into a rabbit! Nothing could be easier – simply replace these ears with the ones in the **Josephine** pattern (see page 43).

repeat 5 more times from * to * (= 42 sts.). The shape of the rose will form naturally (g).

Lock the shape into place by making a few stitches at its base. Make 3 other identical roses.

11. Make the stems. Cut a 20 cm (8") strand of craft wire and fold it in half. Roll brown embroidery thread over the wire, and push the ends of the wire into the bottom center of the rose. Tie off the red and brown threads and weave them in (h). Cut a small kraft paper rectangle in which to wrap the roses.

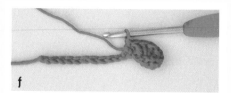

f

g

h

• PORTRAIT OF REYNARD •

Dare to decorate differently with this little crocheted portrait of Reynard the fox. Perfect for a child's room, this pattern is most suited to experienced crocheters, but with a little practice and plenty of motivation, anyone can complete this project.

DIFFICULTY LEVEL ★★★ — DIMENSIONS: 15 X 12 CM (6" X 4.75")

★ Materials

1 ball size 3 tan cotton crochet thread

1 ball size 3 white cotton crochet thread

1 ball size 3 grey cotton crochet thread

1 ball size 3 chartreuse cotton crochet thread

30 cm (11.75") of size 3 black cotton crochet thread

1 ball size 3 silver metallic thread

1 crochet hook – 3.0 mm

2.5 x 10 cm (1" x 4") of tulle

Fat quarter of floral print fabric

Piece of fusible interfacing, same size as the frame

2 plastic safety eyes, black and brown, 6 mm

Basic kit (see page 5)

★ Stitches

Chain stitch (ch)

Single crochet stitch (sc)

Slip stitch (sl st)

Double crochet (dc)

Double treble (dtr)

a

Instructions

1. To make the head, use the white colorway for rounds 1-5, and the tan colorway from round 6-end.

Round 1: ch 2, then add 6 sc in the 1st ch.

Round 2: sc 1, inc 1, sc 2, inc 1, sc 1 (= 8 sc).

Rounds 3-4: sc 1 in each of the 8 sc in previous round (= 8 sc).

Round 5: sc 1, inc 1, sc 1, inc 1, sc 2, inc 1, sc 1 (= 11 sc).

Round 6: change color and sc 1, inc 1, sc 2, inc 1, sc 1, inc 1, sc 2, inc 1, sc 1 (= 15 sc).

Round 7: sc 1, inc 1, sc 2, inc 1, sc 5, inc 1, sc 2, inc 1, sc 1 (= 19 sc).

Round 8: sc 2, inc 1, sc 2, inc 1, sc 7, inc 1, sc 2, inc 1, sc 2 (= 23 sc).

Round 9: sc 1 in each of the 23 sc in previous round (= 23 sc).

Round 10: sc 7, inc 1, sc 7, inc 1, sc 7 (= 25 sc).

Round 11: sc 3, inc 1, sc 4, inc 1, sc 3, inc 1, sc 3, inc 1, sc 4, inc 1, sc 3 (= 30 sc).

Rounds 12-14: sc 1 in each of the 30 sc in previous round (= 30 sc). Clip in the plastic safety eyes at the height of the 13th round, leaving a 7-sc gap between them (see **Creating the Face**, page 11). Thoroughly stuff the head.

Round 15: *sc 3, dec 1*, repeat 5 more times from * to * (= 24 sc).

Round 16: *sc 2, dec 1*, repeat 5 more times from * to * (= 18 sc).

Round 17: *sc 1, dec 1*, repeat 5 more times from * to * (= 12 sc).

Round 18: dec 6 (= 6 sc).

Round 19: sc 3. Finish with 1 sl st. Break yarn, leaving a tail at least 20 cm (8") long, which you will use to attach the head to the frame. Embroider the nose using the black colorway (a).

2. Use the tan colorway to make the torso.

Round 1: ch 2, then add 6 sc in the 1st ch.

Round 2: inc 1 in each sc in previous round (= 12 sc).

Round 3: *sc 1 in next st, inc 1 in next st*, repeat 5 more times from * to * (= 18 sc).

>>

Round 4: sc 1 in each of the 18 sc in previous round (= 18 sc).

Round 5: *sc 2, inc 1*, repeat 5 more times from * to * (= 24 sc).

Round 6: sc 1 in each of the 24 sc in previous round (= 24 sc).

Round 7: *sc 3, inc 1*, repeat 5 more times from * to * (= 30 sc).

Rounds 8-15: sc 1 in each of the 30 sc in previous round (= 30 sc). Line up the edges of your work on top of each other, and work 1 round in sc to close the opening. Make sure you insert the hook in the 2 facing sc stitches (b). Finish with 1 sl st. Break yarn, leaving a 30 cm (11.75") tail to attach the torso to the frame.

Do not stuff. Embroider a few V-shaped decorative stitches with the chartreuse colorway.

3. Use the white and tan colorways to make the ears.

Round 1: with the white colorway, ch

4 and turn, sc 1, dc 1, dtr 1, ch 1 and turn.

Round 2: with the tan colorway, sc 4, ch 1, sc 4. Finish with 1 sl st and break yarn.

Make a second identical ear.

4. Use the grey colorway to make the picture frame. Visually, the frame breaks down into one rectangle with two half-circles at each end. Stitch increases are done in these half-circles, forming the rounded edges of the oval.

Make a chain with ch 12. Work in the round around this chain. These 12 stitches will form the height of the rectangle. Turn your work (the ch 3 at the start of each round count as 1 dc).

Round 1: ch 3, dc 11, dc 6 in the next st (i.e., the 1st ch in the chain), dc 12, dc 6 in the next st (= 36 st). Finish the round with 1 sl st (c).

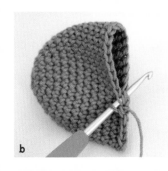

b

Round 2: ch 3, dc 11, *inc 1, dc 1*, repeat 2 more times from * to *, dc 12, *inc 1, dc 1*, repeat 2 more times from * to * (= 42 st). Finish the round with 1 sl st (d).

>>

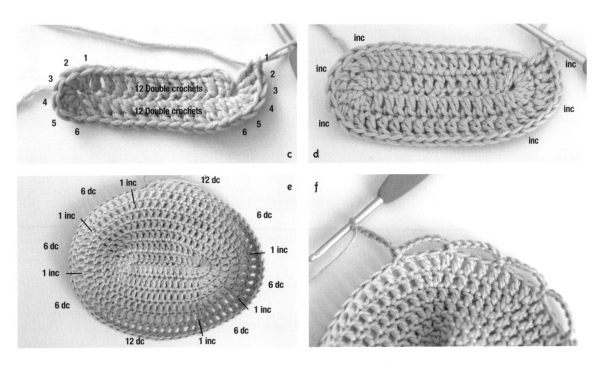

>>

Round 3: ch 3, dc 11, *inc 1, dc 2*, repeat 2 more times from * to *, dc 12, *inc 1, dc 2*, repeat 2 more times from * to * (= 48 st). Finish the round with 1 sl st.

Round 4: ch 3, dc 11, *inc 1, dc 3*, repeat 2 more times from * to *, dc 12, *inc 1, dc 3*, repeat 2 more times from * to * (= 54 st). Finish the round with 1 sl st.

Round 5: ch 3, dc 11, *inc 1, dc 4*, repeat 2 more times from * to *, dc 12, *inc 1, dc 4*, repeat 2 more times from * to * (= 60 st). Finish the round with 1 sl st.

Round 6: ch 3, dc 11, *inc 1, dc 5*, repeat 2 more times from * to *, dc 12, *inc 1, dc 5*, repeat 2 more times from * to * (= 66 st).

Round 7: ch 3, dc 11, *inc 1, dc 6*, repeat 2 more times from * to *, dc 12, *inc 1, dc 6*, repeat 2 more times from * to * (= 72 st). Do not break yarn, as it will be used for edging (e).

5. Make the trim using the same colorway.

Round 1: ch 6, skip 3 st, sl st 1. Repeat this sequence all around the oval.

Round 2: ch 3, sl st 1 into the arc of the circle formed by the ch in the previous round. Next, * ch 6, sl st 1*, repeat this sequence all around the oval. Finish with 1 sl st and break yarn (f).

TIP: *Based on the type of yarn used and individual crochet style (loose or tight gauge), the frame may not be very flat. Should this happen, place it under a heavy dictionary and let it sit overnight.*

Assembly

6. Gather together all pieces for assembly (g). Sew the ears onto the fox's head.

7. Using a tapestry needle, sew the torso onto the frame (h).

g

h

i

j

8. Using the silver thread, make a chain of the same length as the frame oval, without the trim. Use a tapestry needle and the same thread to sew it on, using small running stitches.

9. Sew the fox's head onto the frame (i).

10. Use a piece of tulle to make a small bowtie (see the bowtie instructions for the **Portrait of Olaf** on page 63) and sew it on.

11. Cut a small piece of floral print fabric and a piece of fusible interfacing the same size as the frame oval (without the trim). Use an iron to attach the shiny side of the fusible interfacing to the back of the fabric to stiffen it. Use small running stitches to sew the fabric oval to the back of the frame (j). This step will help stiffen the frame and hide all of the thread tails behind the frame.

Variation

The crocheted frame can be replaced with a fabric frame. To do so, cut an oval from a very thick piece of fusible interfacing, and an equal-sized oval from a piece of floral print or other fabric of your choice. Fuse onto the fabric, using an iron. Sew the head and torso to the center of the resulting frame.

• PORTRAIT OF OLAF •

This pattern is a variation on the **Portrait of Reynard** (page 55). How about starting an entire set of cute family portraits by choosing different outfits and thread colors for each character? Impress your kids and your loved ones by crocheting four or five portraits and then hanging them side by side for a stunning effect!

DIFFICULTY LEVEL: ★★★ — DIMENSIONS: 15 X 12 CM (6" X 4.75")

★ Materials

1 ball size 3 light brown cotton crochet thread
1 ball size 3 white cotton crochet thread
1 ball size 3 grey cotton crochet thread
1 ball size 3 gold metallic thread
Neon pink embroidery thread
Brown embroidery thread
1 crochet hook – 3.0 mm
2.5 x 10 cm (1" x 4") piece of neon pink tulle
Fat quarter of floral print fabric
Piece of fusible interfacing, same size as the frame
2 plastic safety eyes, black and brown, 6 mm
Flexible, thin craft wire
Basic kit (see page 5)

★ Stitches

Chain stitch (ch)
Single crochet stitch (sc)
Slip stitch (sl st)
Double crochet (dc)

Instructions

1. To make the head, use the light brown colorway.

Round 1: ch 2, then add 6 sc in the 1st ch.

Round 2: inc 1 in each sc in previous round (= 12 sc).

Round 3: sc 1, inc 1, sc 8, inc 1, sc 1 (= 14 sc).

Rounds 4-5: sc 1 in each sc in previous round (= 14 sc).

Round 6: sc 1, inc 1, sc 10, inc 1, sc 1 (= 16 sc).

Round 7: sc 1 in each sc in previous round (= 16 sc).

Round 8: sc 5, inc 1, sc 4, inc 1, sc 5 (= 18 sc).

Round 9: sc 1 in each sc in previous round (= 18 sc).

Round 10: sc 1, inc 1, sc 4, inc 1, sc 4, inc 1, sc 4, inc 1, sc 1 (= 22 sc).

Round 11: sc 3, inc 1, sc 14, inc 1, sc 3 (= 24 sc).

Round 12: sc 8, inc 1, sc 6, inc 1, sc 8 (= 26 sc).

Round 13: inc 1, sc 3, inc 1, sc 3, inc 1, sc 4, inc 1, sc 3, inc 1, sc 3, inc 1, sc 3, inc 1 (= 33 sc).

Round 14: sc 10, inc 1, sc 10, inc 1, sc 10, inc 1 (= 36 sc).

Round 15: sc 1 in each of the 36 sc in previous round (= 36 sc).

Round 16: *sc 4, dec 1*, repeat 5 more times from * to * (= 30 sc). Clip in the plastic safety eyes at the height of the 13th round, leaving a 7-sc gap between them, and stuff thoroughly (see **Creating the Face**, page 11).

Round 17: *sc 3, dec 1*, repeat 5 more times from * to * (= 24 sc).

Round 18: *sc 2, dec 1*, repeat 5 more times from * to * (= 18 sc).

Round 19: *sc 1, dec 1*, repeat 5 more times from * to * (= 12 sc).

Round 20: dec 6 (= 6 sc).

>>

>>

Round 21: sc 3. Finish with 1 sl st. Break yarn, leaving a tail at least 20 cm (8") long to attach the head to the frame.

2. Use the white and light brown colorways to make the ears. Make a chain with ch 5 in white, then turn your work.

Round 1: ch 1, sc 1, dc 3, sc 1 (a). Then switch to the light brown colorway and dc 4, dc 3 in the next st to create the curve of the ear, dc 4. Finish with 1 sl st and break yarn (b).

Make a second identical ear.

3. Use the grey colorway to make the torso.

Round 1: ch 2, then add 6 sc in the 1st ch.

Round 2: inc 1 in each sc in previous round (= 12 sc).

Round 3: *sc 1 in next st, inc 1 in next st*, repeat 5 more times from * to * (= 18 sc).

Round 4: sc 1 in each of the 18 sc in previous round (= 18 sc).

Round 5: *sc 2, inc 1*, repeat 5 more times from * to * (= 24 sc).

Round 6: sc 1 in each of the 24 sc in previous round (= 24 sc).

Round 7: *sc 3, inc 1*, repeat 5 more times from * to * (= 30 sc).

Rounds 8-15: sc 1 in each of the 30 sc in previous round (= 30 sc).

Line up the edges of your work on top of each other, and work 1 round in sc to close the opening. Make sure you insert the hook in the 2

facing sc stitches. Finish with 1 sl st. Break yarn, leaving a 30 cm (11.75") tail to attach the torso to the frame. Do not stuff. Use the pink neon thread to embroider a few decorative stitches.

4. Use the white colorway to make the frame and trim. Follow steps 4-5 for the **Portrait of Reynard** pattern (page 57).

Assembly and Finishing

5. Attach the ears to the deer's head (c). If desired, color in the cheeks (see **Creating the Face**, page 11).

6. Using a tapestry needle, sew the torso onto the frame.

7. With the gold thread, make a chain of the same length as the frame oval, without the trim. Use a tapestry needle and the same thread to sew it on, using small running stitches.

8. Sew the deer's head onto the frame.

9. Snip 6 lengths of flexible wire. Join them in groups of 3 (d).

10. To make the deer antlers, wind 50 cm (19.75") of brown embroidery thread around the three lengths of wire (e). When you get close to the end of each stem, fold them in half and continue winding the thread around it to ensure it stays in place (f).

>>

TIP: *These instructions complement those of the Portrait of Reynard (page 55). Consult that chapter to fully understand the various preparation and assembly steps, as described and depicted.*

a

b

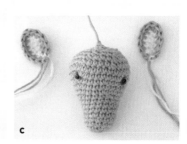

c

>>

11. Insert the antlers at the top of the deer's head. Use a tapestry needle to pull the loose threads into the back of the frame. Knot these together.

12. To make the bowtie, fold the tulle rectangle into an accordion shape. Secure it in the middle by winding a length of neon pink thread. Make a knot and use this thread to sew the bowtie onto the top of the torso (g).

13. Cut a small piece of floral print fabric and a piece of fusible interfacing the same size as the frame oval (without the trim). Use an iron to attach the shiny side of the fusible interfacing to the back of the floral print fabric to stiffen it (h).

14. Use small running stitches to sew the fabric oval to the back of the frame. This step will help stiffen the frame and hide all of the thread tails behind the frame (i).

Variation
The crocheted frame can be replaced with a fabric frame. To do so, cut an oval from a very thick piece of fusible interfacing, and an equal-sized oval from a piece of floral or other fabric of your choice. Fuse the interfacing onto the fabric. Sew the head and torso to the center of the resulting frame.

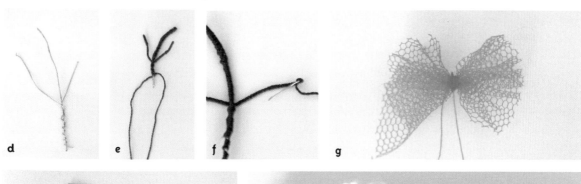

d   e   f   g

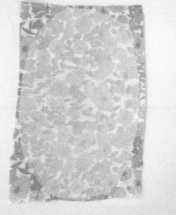

h

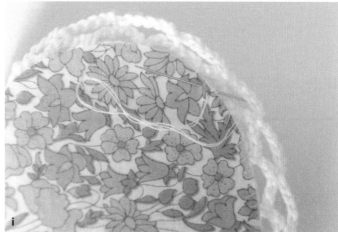

i

Thank you to:

First of all, thank you for picking up this book. I hope that my explanations, along with Caroline Briel's lovely photos, have motivated you to try making some of these little crocheted characters.

I would especially like to thank Nathalie Délimard of the Abracadacraft® site for encouraging me to write this book.

A big thank you to Stéphanie (*Fanette joue à la poupée* blog) and Sarah (*2 clics* blog) for their enthusiasm, advice, and support throughout the birthing of this book.

I would also like to thank my testers, Catherine from the *Petite primprenelle* blog, Patricia from the *Betsy* blog, Isabelle, Claire, and Enna, who undertook these patterns with great care and provided me with invaluable help.

Thank you to my DMC supplier, with whom I was delighted to work to complete this project.

Finally, a wink and a huge thank you to my children Gael, Lisenn, and Louise, as well as their dad, for their patience during the long hours I spent crocheting by their side.

DMC - www.dmc-usa.com, NATURA Just Cotton

You will find a wide range of plastic safety eye clips at craft stores and online from many retailers, including 6060, an online store hosted on the Etsy site (www.etsy.com/shop/6060)

Text and patterns by Sandrine Deveze
Original French title: *Tendre Crochet*
© 2014 Groupe Eyrolles, Paris, France, in partnership with Abracadacraft (www.abracadacraft.com)
Photography and styling by Caroline Briel / CINQMAI (www.carolinebriel.com), step-by-step photography by Sandrine Deveze
Stitch sketches, graphic design, and layout by Julie Simoens

English adaptation by Mady Virgona, © 2015 Peter Pauper Press, Inc.

Published in the United States by Peter Pauper Press, Inc.
202 Mamaroneck Avenue
White Plains, New York, USA 10601

Published in the United Kingdom and Europe by Peter Pauper Press, Inc. c/o White Pebble International
Unit 2, Plot 11 Terminus Rd.
Chichester, West Sussex PO19, 8TX UK

ISBN: 978-1-4413-1836-7
                    Library of Congress Cataloging-in-Publication Data

Deveze, Sandrine.
  {Tendre crochet . English}
  Sweet crochet / by Sandrine Deveze ; photos by Cinqmai.
     pages cm
  Translation of: Tendre crochet.
  ISBN 978-1-4413-1836-7 (pbk. : alk. paper) 1. Soft toys 2. Crocheting--Patterns. I. Title.
  TT174.3 D4813 2015
  74643'4--dc23
                    2014046830

Visit us at www.peterpauper.com